His Journe

His Journey, Our Journey

Daily Reflections from Ash Wednesday to Easter Day

The students and staff of

Ridley Hall CAMBRIDGE

CANTERBURY
PRESS
Norwich

© Ridley Hall 2006

First published in 2006 by the Canterbury Press Norwich
(a publishing imprint of Hymns Ancient & Modern Limited,
a registered charity)
9–17 St Alban's Place, London N1 0NX

www.scm-canterburypress.co.uk

British Library Cataloguing in Publication data

A catalogue record for this book is available
from the British Library

ISBN 1-85311-768-4/978-1-85311-768-8

Typeset by Regent Typesetting, London
Printed and bound by
Bookmarque, Croydon, Surrey

Contents

What readers said about
last year's Lent book

'Your Lent Book has been a great blessing to me. I can relate to its easy understanding, wording and messages.'

'Most striking is the honesty, wisdom and depth with which the contributors write as they open up both the scriptures and their own lives to us. One is left not only with a sense of the Easter hope that dawns at the end of Lent, but also for the future of the church which will be shaped by these gifted and prayerful men and women.'

'An eagerly awaited annual spiritual resource.'

'I am very grateful for the way in which the Lent Book has reached an audience here that does not normally get involved beyond Sunday attendance.'

'There was a wonderful variety of input and the daily challenge benefited by being confined to one page. Priorities seemed right with great compassion and understanding of people and a closeness to Jesus and his Gospel.'

'I would like to thank you once again for giving us fresh and vibrant Lenten reflections.'

Preface

The Ridley Hall Lent Books

Now in their sixth year, the meditations produced by the students at Ridley Hall have become part of the Lenten landscape. It was a tremendous encouragement to the students last year to find their book described as *'an eagerly awaited annual spiritual resource'* within the *Church Times* reviews of the many Lent Books then on offer.

From letters received over the years it seems clear that what differentiates this book from most others published as companions through Lent is the linkage between the Bible passages and the experience of a group of individual 'pilgrims' who happen, at this stage of their lives, to be training to be ministers in the church.

The story of the genesis of these booklets has been told each year but it is well worth repeating. A student, recognizing that the college has a constant need for financial support if it is to grow and improve its facilities, felt concerned that trainee priests (the majority of Ridley students) could seldom give such support. He took the issue to prayer. The feeling grew strongly in him that the practice of writing short meditations based on Bible texts had to be within the grasp of the whole community of Ridley Hall and could be the basis for the students' support for the life of their college.

The idea caught on – or should one say, 'caught fire'? The result was *We Want to See Jesus*, written, assembled and published in five weeks. The enthusiasm of contributors and readers alike laid the foundation for this now annual exercise. Of course, the community membership changes each year with roughly half the members new to the activity. But each year, the new students have joined with the 'returners' and a fresh set of meditations produced. *We Want to Know Christ, The Shame and the Glory, His Story, Our Story* and *I Desire Justice* followed the first experimental book and thousands of copies of each have been distributed.

This year's book is different again. *His Journey, Our Journey* may feel very similar in its title to the 2004 collection but this year the readings are all taken from the one Gospel of Luke and follow the story of our Saviour from the moment he turned his face to Jerusalem until the fateful events of Maundy Thursday, Good Friday and his glorious Resurrection on Easter Day.

Most of us have turbulent times in our lives which demand fortitude and determination; many of us will have felt the tide of events running against us when we are trying to hold to what is good, some of us will have been fortunate enough to have experienced a joy that resonates with the bewildered gladness of the disciples on Easter Day.

You are invited to share the experiences of the current Ridley community of students and staff as you follow the Lord's journey.

We are delighted to once more be making our journeys available to you through the generous collaboration of SCM-Canterbury Press, a practical link we greatly value. If you want to know more about the life of the College where this collection has been shaped, please visit our website (www.ridley.cam.ac.uk).

Foreword by the Principal of Ridley Hall

This Lent Book tells the story of one of the most famous journeys of all time. It is the journey of Jesus of Nazareth, who 'set his face to go to Jerusalem' (Luke 9.51) in order to do nothing less than save the world. But what makes this Lent Book so distinctive is that it also tells of forty-seven other journeys, many of them shared here in print for the first time. These are stories of men and women who in our own time have heard Jesus' call to follow in his way and go where he leads. The course of their journeys through life *now* has changed direction because of Jesus' journey *then*. They have discovered that his journey was one made at great cost for each one of them. It was a journey that reached them and found them and gathered them into the most exciting adventure possible for a human being – a journey into the love of God for the whole world. These are the stories of people who want to encourage others who are already on this journey, and who want to invite anyone who is not already travelling this road to take the risk of stepping out on this great adventure. You will see that the road is not always easy and the going is often tough. But, as you will discover through these honest and moving meditations, it is a journey in which you will never be alone. I am delighted to be able to commend these reflections to you

and I look forward to travelling through Lent with you and
with them.

Christopher Cocksworth
October 2006

Using this Book

In a group

Ridley Hall's students' Lent meditations have proved to be excellent 'starters' for small group discussion. The experience of many groups has been that simply talking about how the prior week's reflections have spoken to group members has been enough to generate conversations and prompt insights that have been highly valued. These have, in turn, built confidence and mutuality, sometimes to an unexpected degree. Our reflection on this is that because the meditations derive from the wide-ranging life experiences of Ridley's students, they easily provoke empathy and establish common ground with the readers. Perhaps this was all summed up best by a church leader who wrote saying, 'With our thanks for a very valuable contribution to our church's life in Lent.'

As an individual

- Each day during Lent, set aside some time in a quiet place. You will need only this book as the relevant Bible passages accompany each reflection.
- Do whatever helps you to relax – sit somewhere quiet, make a drink, take some deep breaths.
- Pray for God's guidance before you read; the scripture passage on page 1 might help.

- Read the Bible passage set for the day, and think about what it might be saying.
- Then read the reflection for the day, slowly, and pause for thought as you go. How does it relate to the Bible passage? Is there anything in the reflection which is similar to or different from anything you have experienced or thought before?
- When you have read and reflected, pray about what you have read and ask God if he might be speaking to you through it; you might like to use the Lord's Prayer to finish.

The Daily Reflections

O send out your light and your truth;
let them lead me;
let them bring me to your holy hill
and to your dwelling.
Then will I go to the altar of God,
to God my exceeding joy;
and I will praise you with the harp,
O God, my God.

Psalm 43.3

Luke 9.51–56

When the days drew near for him to be taken up, he set his face to go to Jerusalem. And he sent messengers ahead of him. On their way they entered a village of the Samaritans to make ready for him; but they did not receive him, because his face was set toward Jerusalem. When his disciples James and John saw it, they said, 'Lord, do you want us to command fire to come down from heaven and consume them?' But he turned and rebuked them. Then they went on to another village.

The journey begins. It is a journey of purpose and focus. Jesus sets off resolutely to go towards Jerusalem, his death, resurrection, and beyond to establish a story of salvation for all. There is no indecisiveness in his course of action. But it is a journey that takes some unusual twists, at times in surprising directions that are not the easy way. As we will see over the coming weeks, Jesus does not take the usual route to Jerusalem, and, for some chapters to come, we will find him in and around Galilee.

We all remember journeys we have taken. The perennial problems of reading maps, attempting to take short cuts and getting lost come to mind! Similarly in the story of our lives to date, we can think of times when the journey has been longer than expected because God wanted us to take that route to accomplish some particular purpose. At other times, we have chosen to take the longer route because of our sin, or through short-sightedness. Also, if we are honest, there are times when we have tried to take the short route and just got completely lost. Like the disciples, we can be tempted to let the resulting frustration get the better of us.

This passage is the first mention in Luke's Gospel of the story of Jesus' journey to Jerusalem. As we start our journey through Lent, is there a particular purpose that our lives are focused towards? Where are you headed?

Father God, at the beginning of this period of Lent, be our guide and focus as we walk through the journey of life.

Luke 9.57–62

As they were going along the road, someone said to him, 'I will follow you wherever you go.' And Jesus said to him, 'Foxes have holes, and birds of the air have nests; but the Son of Man has nowhere to lay his head.' To another he said, 'Follow me.' But he said, 'Lord, first let me go and bury my father.' But Jesus said to him, 'Let the dead bury their own dead; but as for you, go and proclaim the kingdom of God.' Another said, 'I will follow you, Lord; but let me first say farewell to those at my home.' Jesus said to him, 'No one who puts a hand to the plough and looks back is fit for the kingdom of God.'

I like to think I'm not the only person to have made promises to 'be there' for friends – only to feel foolish and guilty when I fail to follow or support them as I had pledged to do. It isn't always easy following Jesus either, as he makes clear in this passage from Luke's Gospel. There are some 'hard sayings' here. If I take Jesus seriously I may be asked to leave home and loved ones behind for the sake of the kingdom of God. Maybe that is why when I first felt the nudges of a call to ministry I said to my chaplain, 'David, I'm scared!' 'Yes,' he replied, 'You should be!' But he smiled as he said this.

A few years later (on a wing and a prayer!) I left a beautiful island, friends, and the security of a 'known' life – feeling rather envious of foxes and birds of the air. Yet on those occasions when I *have* followed obediently and without looking back as I ploughed ahead, I have found myself surprised. Surprised by the beauty of the journey, and the joy of new friends along the way. Wonderful though these things are, an even deeper joy comes from drawing closer to Jesus as far as I am able, for as long as I am able – and yes, I'm still scared as I say that, but this time I'm the one who is smiling!

May God make our path clear and hold us in his hands as we journey.

Luke 10.1–4

After this the Lord appointed seventy others and sent them on ahead of him in pairs to every town and place where he himself intended to go. He said to them, 'The harvest is plentiful, but the labourers are few; therefore ask the Lord of the harvest to send out labourers into his harvest. Go on your way. See, I am sending you out like lambs into the midst of wolves. Carry no purse, no bag, no sandals; and greet no one on the road.'

'After this . . .' After, that is, establishing that following Jesus is costly and affects every allegiance. Only now does Jesus appoint these seventy followers to spread the life-changing message of God's kingdom. He sends them in pairs, a reminder that they work best not alone but as part of a team. They need the encouragement of fellow labourers; created by a relational God they can only be fulfilled human beings working alongside others in serving him.

You and I are Christ's 'labourers' of today, and we are called not only to share the good news of Jesus, but also to pray for more fellow labourers through whom God's full harvest will come. It *is* plentiful. Jesus does indeed long to bring our friends and families, our communities and nations, into his kingdom. Our task is urgent; there is no time for dallying on the road.

This task will not be easy, for we too are sent out 'like lambs into the midst of wolves'. Risky this may be, and dangerous. But foolish and suicidal? Not at all. For Jesus the Good Shepherd is our strength, and we are his sheep, to whom he promises protection even from the snares of the world and the devil. Therefore, go. Bring in the harvest!

Lord Jesus, give us grace to work together and to pray for more labourers for your kingdom.

Luke 10.17–20

The seventy returned with joy, saying, 'Lord, in your name even the demons submit to us!' He said to them, 'I watched Satan fall from heaven like a flash of lightning. See, I have given you authority to tread on snakes and scorpions, and over all the power of the enemy; and nothing will hurt you. Nevertheless, do not rejoice at this, that the spirits submit to you, but rejoice that your names are written in heaven.'

Are we to be surprised by seeing God act to change lives, as these seventy seemed to be? Is it something done solely by experts or that only occurs at slick, well-attended events with freshly ground coffee and a homely atmosphere? We live in a society crying out for the Gospel, but are we dozing in a subculture that believes that it's someone else's job to actually share it?

After years of vague spiritual searching and kidding myself that I was OK, I finally became a Christian five years ago at one such welcoming event. One of the obstacles that I feared to face soon after was the challenge of 'sharing my faith with a friend'. But I knew I had to do it, so I prayed for courage and got on with it. My approach has often comprised listening to stories of hurt or loss or confusion and highlighting ways that I'm just like my friend or colleague. I can share in the experience of being broken as I recall how far I strayed from the path of Christ. Often stories are swapped about how meaningless things can appear to be when there is so much inequality, injustice and suffering in the world.

And that's where I could leave it, if not for God's promise that my name is written in heaven in the handwriting of a loving father. As I share that sense of homecoming, of belonging, I have seen my listener transformed little by little into someone who wants to come home too, and one more enters the kingdom. One more enemy stronghold falls.

Lord, give us courage, compassion and wisdom to profess your truth openly and with boldness.

Luke 10.21–24

At that same hour Jesus rejoiced in the Holy Spirit and said, 'I thank you, Father, Lord of heaven and earth, because you have hidden these things from the wise and the intelligent and have revealed them to infants; yes, Father, for such was your gracious will. All things have been handed over to me by my Father; and no one knows who the Son is except the Father, or who the Father is except the Son and anyone to whom the Son chooses to reveal him.'

Then turning to the disciples, Jesus said to them privately, 'Blessed are the eyes that see what you see! For I tell you that many prophets and kings desired to see what you see, but did not see it, and to hear what you hear, but did not hear it.'

On a mountain overlooking the whole of Rio de Janeiro is a statue of Christ with arms wide open. It's called 'Christo Redontor' ('Christ the Redeemer'). I'm not a particular fan of statues, but this image will live with me forever. Rio gave me a fascinating glimpse of the extremes of our fallen world: fantastic natural beauty contrasting with the human mess and pollution, extreme wealth and extreme poverty literally side by side and both very obvious, a very welcoming and friendly people but real problems of violence and corruption in society. But there overlooking it all is Christ the Redeemer, Christ who has journeyed to the cross on behalf of this fallen world, reaching out with open arms ready to embrace those who choose to turn back to God. Sometimes low clouds or fog can obscure the statue. But it's still there.

These verses from Luke remind us that it is not through learning, wisdom or privilege of position that people can see God the Father or know who he is, but through grace and a childlike faith in Jesus. Many are blind to this in a world that refuses to see. But Jesus, having chosen in obedience to his Father to bring reconciliation through his death and resurrection, is there with arms outstretched in love, longing for all to receive his gift. He wants to embrace people and bring them into an eternal relationship with God our Father, that they may join us on his path through the cross to life.

Father, thank you for Jesus' wide open arms of welcome and love. Give grace to your world and open the eyes of everyone to see the fullness of what Christ has accomplished for us.

Luke 10.25–28

Just then a lawyer stood up to test Jesus. 'Teacher,' he said, 'what must I do to inherit eternal life?' He said to him, 'What is written in the law? What do you read there?' He answered, 'You shall love the Lord your God with all your heart, and with all your soul, and with all your strength, and with all your mind; and your neighbour as yourself.' And he said to him, 'You have given the right answer; do this, and you will live.'

I once heard someone say, 'If you're having trouble loving someone then just *love them*.' Sounds simple, doesn't it? We all have the capacity to love someone but it is just so hard sometimes. How can we love those who appear un-lovable, those who are different from us, those people we don't like?

God's very nature is to love, but the kind of love he calls us to is, for us, a choice, a response to his love that requires all that we are. Most people think love is a feeling, an emotion that comes and goes, and they confuse loving with liking. But the love referred to in our passage is not about mushy feelings but about concrete actions, especially when we may not feel like it.

How then should we love those around us? Can we remember what it's like to be loved and apply that to our neighbour? To the troubled teenager next door? To the work colleague who gets up our nose? To the paedophile who lives in the next street?

We can't do it on our own. Jesus loved the unlovable but he also prayed to God for help. Remembering his love for us, we *can* take steps (even if they are small ones) to demonstrate love, with the help of the Holy Spirit. Perhaps the first step is to pray and ask God to bless that person – without our conditions!

Loving Lord, we pray to you because we cannot truly love without you. Help us to love our neighbour as we love ourselves.

Luke 10.29–37

But wanting to justify himself, he (a lawyer) asked Jesus, 'And who is my neighbour?'

Jesus replied, 'A man was going down from Jerusalem to Jericho, and fell into the hands of robbers, who stripped him, beat him, and went away, leaving him half dead. Now by chance a priest was going down that road; and when he saw him, he passed by on the other side. So likewise a Levite, when he came to the place and saw him, passed by on the other side. But a Samaritan while travelling came near him; and when he saw him, he was moved with pity. He went to him and bandaged his wounds, having poured oil and wine on them. Then he put him on his own animal, brought him to an inn, and took care of him. The next day he took out two denarii, gave them to the innkeeper, and said, 'Take care of him; and when I come back, I will repay you whatever more you spend.' Which of these three, do you think, was a neighbour to the man who fell into the hands of the robbers?' He said, 'The one who showed him mercy.' Jesus said to him, 'Go and do likewise.'

Have you ever been 'moved with pity'? If you're anything like me, you may have felt sorry for a poor, small furry creature bewildered by your car headlights, so you swerved to miss it and let it live to dice with death another day. Or maybe you've felt a pang of guilt when images depicting starving children in a far-off country crept up on you during the ad break of a favourite sit-com, so you rang the number, made a contribution, felt better and got back to the show. But what about profound pity, the kind that grabs you and *moves* you with compassion? The pity of the Samaritan that the Worldwide English New Testament describes as wanting 'to *share* in his troubles'?

One summer I was in Malawi with my fiancée and her mother. Speeding along an empty highway we came across a horrific accident. An overcrowded minibus had driven off the road and flipped over into a ditch. It was chaos. My mother-in-law-to-be leapt into action and began to organize and attend to victims, but I froze with fear. All I could think about was the blood and the prevalence of HIV, malaria and hepatitis. Pity was the furthest thing from my mind.

Jesus teaches us that to be a neighbour is to be moved with pity *and* into action. To see the battered, bloodied individual as not just a problem; to cross barriers of prejudice and fear; to get our hands dirty; to allow the stranger into our personal space; and to give generously of our time and money.

Lord, give me grace to be a true neighbour.

Luke 10.38–42

Now as they went on their way, he entered a certain village, where a woman named Martha welcomed him into her home. She had a sister named Mary, who sat at the Lord's feet and listened to what he was saying. But Martha was distracted by her many tasks; so she came to him and asked, 'Lord, do you not care that my sister has left me to do all the work by myself? Tell her then to help me.' But the Lord answered her, 'Martha, Martha, you are worried and distracted by many things; there is need of one thing. Mary has chosen the better part, which will not be taken away from her.'

I think I should start with a confession – I'm a 'Martha'. And I think that Martha gets a bit of a raw deal in this story. After all, someone needed to be doing the cooking, didn't they? Someone needed to be doing all the little jobs that meant the household could offer Jesus the hospitality that he deserved. And anyway, the cooking was an expression of Martha's love for Jesus, wasn't it?

Perhaps, like me, you recognize yourself in the character of Martha. Well, the good news is that there's nothing wrong with being busy, or responding to God, just as Isaiah did, with the words, 'Here I am, send me!' The problem comes when our activity is all-consuming, when 'getting the job done' becomes more important than the One that we're doing it for. It's too easy to fall into activity for activity's sake; to keep doing what we're doing because we've always done it, or because that's what others expect of us. Time spent in prayer, at the feet of Jesus, doesn't have the same measurable success criteria, so it's easy for it to get squeezed out of our task-oriented lives and communities.

I believe that God loves the 'Martha' in me, that he loves it when I am busy being an activist in his name. But he calls me too to sit with Mary, at Jesus' feet; to love him and to let him love me. It's there that I hear his gentle reminder that before I *do* anything, I am his precious child.

Lord, teach me how to receive from you, as well as how to give.

Luke 11.1–4

He was praying in a certain place, and after he had finished, one of his disciples said to him, 'Lord, teach us to pray, as John taught his disciples.' He said to them, 'When you pray, say:

> Father, Hallowed be your name.
> Your kingdom come.
> Give us each day our daily bread.
> And forgive us our sins,
> For we ourselves forgive everyone indebted to us.
> And do not bring us to the time of trial.'

Words, even wonderful words, can grow too familiar. For us, these familiar words can become a refrain, a chant, or simply a familiar point in a formal service; words said on autopilot.

Wherever we are in relation to these words, today we have an opportunity to stop, look, and explore the significance of this moment to the disciples.

The disciple asked Jesus to teach them to pray. We might imagine the disciples sitting, waiting for Jesus to finish his praying. What caused them to ask? They would all have been taught to pray by their fathers and mothers. They would have received the traditions from the synagogue, and been to the Temple in Jerusalem. Some or all of them would have seen John, and he had taught a prayer to his disciples.

What would Jesus say? They would have seen his devotion, going out early alone to pray, and his dependence upon those times. Perhaps they realized that prayer was the key to his life, to all he did.

Saying 'Abba, Father' was intimate in a way which set a new tone. They would all have known God as the Father of the nation, the one who led his people Israel through the wilderness, and the great and holy God who delivered them out of the hand of the oppressor. Here Jesus uses this personal word for 'my father'. This was completely new, and each subsequent phrase acts as a door to another world of prayer. The disciples could now join with Jesus in prayer. Through this prayer that Jesus taught, we too can learn to pray as he did.

Lord Jesus, move us to take up this invitation to pray as you did, and to see what you saw.

Luke 11.5–13

And he said to them, 'Suppose one of you has a friend, and you go to him at midnight and say to him, "Friend, lend me three loaves of bread; for a friend of mine has arrived, and I have nothing to set before him." And he answers from within, "Do not bother me; the door has already been locked, and my children are with me in bed; I cannot get up and give you anything." I tell you, even though he will not get up and give him anything because he is his friend, at least because of his persistence he will get up and give him whatever he needs.

So I say to you, Ask, and it will be given to you; search, and you will find; knock, and the door will be opened for you. For everyone who asks receives, and everyone who searches finds, and for everyone who knocks, the door will be opened. Is there anyone among you who, if your child asks for a fish, will give a snake instead of a fish? Or if the child asks for an egg, will give a scorpion? If you then, who are evil, know how to give good gifts to your children, how much more will the heavenly Father give the Holy Spirit to those who ask him!'

Every boy growing up knows that there are really only two types of pet that are worth having: a snake or a scorpion. Try as I might, I could never convince my dad to buy me either. It would seem that the disciples had a similar problem when it came to approaching God, they weren't sure how to approach him and they weren't sure what to say. Before this passage they ask Jesus to teach them how to pray. Jesus gave them a prayer to pray and, then here, a way to pray it.

What Jesus says is remarkable. The point of his story is not that God is like a sleeping neighbour, who will eventually, frustrated and tired, get up and give us what we need. God is more than a neighbour or a friend, he is our Father, and is waiting and willing to meet our requests. We might feel nervous about waking our neighbours up in the early hours of the morning to beg them for a favour; such nervous trepidation need never affect our prayers because of the relationship we have with God. When we pray we can confidently approach Father God knowing he wants to give us the good gifts that we need.

Just as fathers the world over recognize that snakes and young children are not a happy combination, our Father knows what is best for us: there is no such thing as unanswered prayer. Jesus leaves us with the important reminder that our relationship with God means that the best thing we can ask for is his very presence, in the person of his Holy Spirit.

Father, thank you that we can confidently come to you with our needs. Give us perseverance in prayer, and grant us the guidance of your Spirit.

Luke 11.29–32

When the crowds were increasing, he began to say, 'This generation is an evil generation; it asks for a sign, but no sign will be given to it except the sign of Jonah. For just as Jonah became a sign to the people of Nineveh, so the Son of Man will be to this generation. The queen of the South will rise at the judgement with the people of this generation and condemn them, because she came from the ends of the earth to listen to the wisdom of Solomon, and see, something greater than Solomon is here! The people of Nineveh will rise up at the judgement with this generation and condemn it, because they repented at the proclamation of Jonah, and see, something greater than Jonah is here!'

A busy town centre, a network of roads, a modern super-market – all are full of signs.

As a generation we are comfortable with signs. We want to be shown clearly where we are going and to know exactly what is happening. We find security in this knowledge and complain when there is insufficient or misleading direction. Without it we are anxious that things are slipping from our control, and we feel lost.

Jesus too encountered a generation that desired signs, clear signs from God. Jesus, however, would offer no dramatic sign, for the words he preached and the actions he performed were sufficient. And so he reminded them of the prophecy of Jonah to the people of Nineveh, and the deep wisdom of Solomon. The people of Nineveh and the Queen of Sheba, though they were Gentiles, recognized truth in the words of Jonah and Solomon. The generation who stood before Jesus could, if they but looked, see someone even greater in prophetic power and godly wisdom. But instead of listening and repenting, they asked for proof on their own terms.

In this Lent period, let us train our senses not to look for worldly signs but to hear afresh the words of the one who did far more than remain, as Jonah did, three days and three nights in a creature's belly. We worship one who truly died, was buried, and lay in the belly of the earth for three days, and rose to ensure us a certain future. His name is Jesus.

Lord Jesus, grant us ears to hear and feet to follow you readily on the journey you set before us.

Luke 12.4–7

'I tell you, my friends, do not fear those who kill the body, and after that can do nothing more. But I will warn you whom to fear: fear him who, after he has killed, has authority to cast into hell. Yes, I tell you, fear him! Are not five sparrows sold for two pennies? Yet not one of them is forgotten in God's sight. But even the hairs of your head are all counted. Do not be afraid; you are of more value than many sparrows.'

This passage has two very different parts: a rather nasty reference to hell, and a rather nice bit about sparrows. We would like Jesus only to have said one of them, but this would be a mistake, for the two go together like peas in a pod.

Jesus begins by saying we should not fear those who would harm our bodies but instead fear God who can condemn our souls. Fear in the Bible doesn't always mean raw terror; it can also mean reverence and awe. Fear of God is the beginning of wisdom, something wholly positive that leads to obedience. To fear God is to recognize that his power is far greater than any human threat we may confront. If they can hurt us, like Aslan he *could* do much worse!

But that's not his intention, in the light of what Jesus says next. The Creator of the universe remembers even one sparrow, and he values us much more than many sparrows. Just as a sparrow is worth very little in pounds sterling, so we often feel of little worth to God. But his value system is not like ours, and we know he cares for us because he has demonstrated his power and given us the greatest gift of all in his only Son, Jesus Christ.

O Lord who will never forget us, and who strengthens us in our hour of need, be with all those who are afraid, and help them to know your comfort and strength to deliver.

Luke 12.8–12

'And I tell you, everyone who acknowledges me before others, the Son of Man also will acknowledge before the angels of God; but whoever denies me before others will be denied before the angels of God. And everyone who speaks a word against the Son of Man will be forgiven; but whoever blasphemes against the Holy Spirit will not be forgiven. When they bring you before the synagogues, the rulers, and the authorities, do not worry about how you are to defend yourselves or what you are to say; for the Holy Spirit will teach you at that very hour what you ought to say.'

When I was working in mental health care I often came across people engaged in some kind of spiritual struggle. To be a person of faith employed in this setting is both a privilege and an immense challenge. It was especially difficult to deal with the cynicism of some people who work with the mentally unwell. I can recall more than one occasion when I joined a colleague in accusing 'the church' and organized religion in general for 'allowing' someone to become mentally distressed by encouraging them to believe in a God who loves people to feel guilty and will tolerate nothing less than perfection. Far from acknowledging the Son of Man, I spent a lot of time denying him and undermining his purposes.

Much of this grew from my lack of confidence. I hadn't fully grasped the crucial importance of knowing a God who forgives our failures and invites us to think outside of our context and see the bigger picture. It was incredible and humbling to realize that God had forgiven me for my part in increasing the mental suffering of others. But of course it is also obvious, or should have been to me. As I began to trust the words of this passage, I was able to speak God's truth both to colleagues and to bosses, without being fearful that I would be judged and labelled as those we cared for had been judged. As we begin to acknowledge God, so he can begin to use us to stand up for the vulnerable and persecuted.

Lord, help us always to acknowledge you as our saviour and as a friend to all.

Luke 12.13–21

Someone in the crowd said to him, 'Teacher, tell my brother to divide the family inheritance with me.' But he said to him, 'Friend, who set me to be a judge or arbitrator over you?' And he said to them, 'Take care! Be on your guard against all kinds of greed; for one's life does not consist in the abundance of possessions.' Then he told them a parable: 'The land of a rich man produced abundantly. And he thought to himself, "What should I do, for I have no place to store my crops?" Then he said, "I will do this: I will pull down my barns and build larger ones, and there I will store all my grain and my goods. And I will say to my soul, Soul, you have ample goods laid up for many years; relax, eat, drink, be merry." But God said to him, "You fool! This very night your life is being demanded of you. And the things you have prepared, whose will they be?" So it is with those who store up treasures for themselves but are not rich towards God.'

At first glance, this passage seems to belong to that theme of God versus Mammon which Jesus so often revisits, with images of camels and needles and so on. On this occasion it's a man building barns, but a significant point appears at the very beginning of Jesus' story: 'The land of a rich man produced abundantly'. The man in the story is celebrating a God-given, massive harvest; the problem is what he chooses to do with it, cramming it into barns in the hope that it will last for years to come. His downfall does not come from being rich, but from being naïve enough to think that he can keep it all, unspoiled, for himself.

Similarly, the Israelites in the wilderness were particularly warned against storing any of their manna food overnight. If they did, it rotted. It was God's warning against greed, his provision against one Israelite being better off than the next, and also his encouragement that they were to rely on him, morning by morning, for all they needed. The parable of the man building barns is tucked in among several passages in which Jesus emphasizes the need to rely on God.

Which of God's abundant gifts do we build barns for, hoping to preserve them and keep them just for our own use? Relationships, personalities, talents or possessions – if we keep them hidden in barns for ourselves, for whatever reason, the rot sets in. Let's be generous and daring with the gifts God gives us – and rely on him to renew them just as richly.

Lord, guard us from selfishness, and help us to reflect your generosity and grace in our lives.

Luke 12.22–31

He said to his disciples, 'Therefore I tell you, do not worry about your life, what you will eat, or about your body, what you will wear. For life is more than food, and the body more than clothing. Consider the ravens: they neither sow nor reap, they have neither storehouse nor barn, and yet God feeds them. Of how much more value are you than the birds! And can any of you by worrying add a single hour to your span of life? If then you are not able to do so small a thing as that, why do you worry about the rest? Consider the lilies, how they grow: they neither toil nor spin; yet I tell you, even Solomon in all his glory was not clothed like one of these. But if God so clothes the grass of the field, which is alive today and tomorrow is thrown into the oven, how much more will he clothe you – you of little faith! And do not keep striving for what you are to eat and what you are to drink, and do not keep worrying. For it is the nations of the world that strive after all these things, and your Father knows that you need them. Instead, strive for his kingdom, and these things will be given to you as well.'

Whenever I read this passage in Luke's Gospel, Bobby McFerrin's popular song leaps uninvited into my head. I hum along silently to myself, and then break out into the whistling section aloud – attracting puzzled looks from anyone nearby. (When reading in church I have to exercise saintly restraint.)

Its lyrics, with their memorable refrain 'Don't worry, be happy', begin to explain the theme of this passage. Over recent years there has been a spate of books published on happiness. It appears that happiness is elusive and fleeting, and any advice on how to find and keep it is eagerly sought. Modern medicine is conclusive regarding the dangers of worrying. Stress is firmly linked with a whole host of health problems, and is almost certain to affect a person's life expectancy. Of course Jesus knew this, even without our modern medicine. Can worry add a single hour to our lives?

A popular saying tells us that 'Happiness depends on our circumstances, but joy depends on our heart.' If our *aim* is simply happiness, we may find that just as some circumstances bring happiness, so others may bring worry. Rather, we seek first the kingdom of God, which St Paul tells us is one of peace and joy in the Holy Spirit (Romans 14.7).

There is simply no point in trying to control our own levels of worry or happiness. We, with all creation, are under God's loving care and provision. To paraphrase the Westminster Confession: 'The first purpose of humans is to glorify God and enjoy Him forever.' It is fulfilling this purpose upon which our joy depends, and by which our worries are dispelled.

Lord Jesus, help us to bring our anxieties to you and to know the joy that comes from seeking first your kingdom.

Luke 12.32–34

'Do not be afraid, little flock, for it is your Father's good pleasure to give you the kingdom. Sell your possessions, and give alms. Make purses for yourselves that do not wear out, an unfailing treasure in heaven, where no thief comes near and no moth destroys. For where your treasure is, there your heart will be also.'

'A budget is a moral document.' I first heard this phrase used by Jim Wallis a few years ago, at a conference. Jim is editor of *Sojourners* magazine and an eloquent, passionate commentator on the political environment and the relationship between faith, politics and justice. And it's true, isn't it? Whatever we may say we believe in or support, our true values will be evident from where we choose to invest our resources, be they our time, our money or our possessions.

Jesus observes, 'Where your treasure is, there your heart will be also', challenging us to look honestly at what our priorities truly are, where our security really lies and to consider the things in which we are really putting our faith. He invites us to invest in something that will last for eternity. He calls us to trust and not to be afraid; to put our trust in a generous God, rather than material possessions, social status or worldly recognition.

Where and how will we make our own investment in the kingdom of God? Some of us may be called to be entrepreneurs; high-risk investors taking God's work into new areas. Some of us will be called to invest in seemingly low-risk, low-return ventures, but where steady and faithful endurance over the long term are needed. The question is not whether to invest or not but 'What kind of investor will you be?' Where will your heart be?

Father, help me to find my true security in you and not in the things you have given me. Free me from fear, so that I may be generous with your resources; show me where and how to invest in the things of eternal significance.

Luke 12.35–40

'Be dressed for action and have your lamps lit; be like those who are waiting for their master to return from the wedding banquet, so that they may open the door for him as soon as he comes and knocks. Blessed are those slaves whom the master finds alert when he comes; truly I tell you, he will fasten his belt and have them sit down to eat, and he will come and serve them. If he comes during the middle of the night, or near dawn, and finds them so, blessed are those slaves.

But know this: if the owner of the house had known at what hour the thief was coming, he would not have let his house be broken into. You also must be ready, for the Son of Man is coming at an unexpected hour.'

DAY 17 – WEEK 3 – FRIDAY

It is very easy to be preoccupied with the 'busy-ness' of life. When I reach the end of a day I often realise how small a part I have allowed God in it. As part of our formation as Christians and priests at Ridley, we meet once or twice a term for a one-on-one with the chaplain. Invariably we are asked 'And how is your prayer life?' This is the question to ask if you wish to disconcert clergy and ordinands. One reason for asking it is to make us realize how we are oriented – do we fit our lives around God, or fit God into our lives?

The servants know that their master will return . . . but when? They anticipate his return by having their lights already lit. They are looking at the door, waiting, straining to hear the footsteps outside, ready to open it. They fit their other tasks around this most important person in their lives.

We too live in the tension that our master may return at any time. The oil that burns in our lamps is prayer, fuel for the light of Christ working in and through us by the Holy Spirit. How easy it is to quench this light by unrepentant hearts and by neglecting prayer. As the servants no doubt did, let us support each other to stay awake. But may we also live in a state of anticipation, focused on God through prayer as we look for our master's sudden and glorious arrival, and our invitation to the feast.

Lord of Glory, help us to keep our lamps burning, to be prepared day by day for your return. Transform us by your loving grace that we may delight in living in anticipation of your return.

Luke 12.41–48

Peter said, 'Lord, are you telling this parable for us or for everyone?' And the Lord said, 'Who then is the faithful and prudent manager whom his master will put in charge of his slaves, to give them their allowance of food at the proper time? Blessed is that slave whom his master will find at work when he arrives. Truly I tell you, he will put that one in charge of all his possessions. But if that slave says to himself, "My master is delayed in coming", and if he begins to beat the other slaves, men and women, and to eat and drink and get drunk, the master of that slave will come on a day when he does not expect him and at an hour that he does not know, and will cut him in pieces, and put him with the unfaithful. That slave who knew what his master wanted, but did not prepare himself or do what was wanted, will receive a severe beating. But one who did not know and did what deserved a beating will receive a light beating. From everyone to whom much has been given, much will be required; and from one to whom much has been entrusted, even more will be demanded.'

What a contrast! Here Jesus sets out two alternative scenarios, a steward who is faithful to his master and one who abuses his position. The position Jesus has in mind is *oikonomos*, the household manager who had an important role in managing people, distributing resources and organizing what went on. It is fascinating that in verses 43, 45 and 47 the manager is then described as a 'slave'. The variation of title emphasizes his dual relationship – he both possessed authority (over the manservants and maidservants) and was under authority (to the master).

Stewardship is the state of being responsible for things that belong to another. Many of us find ourselves in a role of middle management. We are accountable to someone above us, whether that be a chief executive, a line manager, or an office supervisor. We need to be loyal, trustworthy and competent. We also work alongside staff who look to us, not just for daily provisions – a food allowance – but for direction, support and encouragement. We should not be like the rogue in the parable who wasted resources and abused power.

But the model of stewardship also applies to the big picture – our relationship with God. God has made humans stewards or managers of his creation. The extent of the current ecological crisis shows how poorly we have discharged that responsibility. Furthermore, God has given each one of us particular gifts, to use for his service and glory in the world and in the church. Are we using, developing and harnessing our own gifts? And are we using, developing and harnessing the gifts of other people?

Lord Jesus, help me to heed your solemn warning, and to be a faithful steward of all that you have entrusted to me.

Luke 12.49–53

'I came to bring fire to the earth, and how I wish it were already kindled! I have a baptism with which to be baptized, and what stress I am under until it is completed! Do you think that I have come to bring peace to the earth? No, I tell you, but rather division! From now on, five in one household will be divided, three against two and two against three; they will be divided:

father against son
 and son against father,
mother against daughter
 and daughter against mother,
mother-in-law against her daughter-in-law
 and daughter-in-law against mother-in-law.'

I remember watching the first *Star Wars* film nearly thirty years ago one wet Saturday afternoon in Canterbury, surrounded by children and a few parents. And it was magic! I've since seen the rest of the saga; sequels and 'prequels', on the big screen and on the small screen in my living room. The story begins by following the journey of Anakin Skywalker as he grows up. Later in the saga he chooses to use the amazing power of the 'force' for his own purposes and, by doing so, corrupts himself. Anakin Skywalker transforms into Darth Vader, one of the bad guys eventually defeated by the hero.

The *Star Wars* story is fiction, thankfully, but it is a dramatic reminder that we all have to make the same choice as Anakin. Do we commit ourselves to a life focused on ourselves? Or do we choose to follow Jesus in a life in which the other is more important than ourselves?

This not just a philosophical debate. In today's difficult passage Jesus tells us he brings the destructive and refining power of fire, and that we will be held to account. He warns that a result of his coming is not peace but division, even within families – the most intimate of our social groups.

Anakin Skywalker made a poor choice, setting himself against the hero, who is his son. In calling us, Jesus asks us to declare our allegiance. Are we truly with Christ? Or against him?

Loving Lord, give us the courage to follow you in spite of painful opposition.

Luke 13.10–17

Now he was teaching in one of the synagogues on the sabbath. And just then there appeared a woman with a spirit that had crippled her for eighteen years. She was bent over and was quite unable to stand up straight. When Jesus saw her, he called her over and said, 'Woman, you are set free from your ailment.' When he laid his hands on her, immediately she stood up straight and began praising God. But the leader of the synagogue, indignant because Jesus had cured on the sabbath, kept saying to the crowd, 'There are six days on which work ought to be done; come on those days and be cured, and not on the sabbath day.' But the Lord answered him and said, 'You hypocrites! Does not each of you on the sabbath untie his ox or his donkey from the manger, and lead it away to give it water? And ought not this woman, a daughter of Abraham whom Satan bound for eighteen long years, be set free from this bondage on the sabbath day?' When he said this, all his opponents were put to shame; and the entire crowd was rejoicing at all the wonderful things that he was doing.

I had been that way for eighteen years. I guess I had got used to it, almost accepted it: the constant aches and pains, not sleeping well at night, the jibes of kids in the village, seeing their dusty feet kicking my stick away. Part of me seemed to have died inside: the result of years of always looking down, never seeing a bird wheeling across the sky or the sun that cast its shadows around my feet. Eighteen years since I had been able to look someone in the eye, to see their smile, to allow them to see my face and read my feelings. Twisted outside and inside. Nobody seemed to notice me. It didn't matter. I didn't matter.

But then the rabbi, the one they call Jesus came to our synagogue. He noticed. He stopped for me. Called me. I felt his strong hands touch my back. I felt the authority of his voice, 'You are set free.' Embarrassment and shame were overcome by a desire to look up into his face. I slowly straightened and my stick fell to the ground. My eyes met the eyes of Jesus. They found recognition, acceptance, and love. Joy welled up within from my feet to my head: 'Praise God! I am free!' My cry was taken up by the crowd, strangers whose faces I now turned to see. This Daughter of Abraham was set free by God to share in the promises of his new kingdom.

Lord, help us to know your freedom and to bring your freedom from bondage to all who are stooped and bowed down.

Luke 13.18–21

He said therefore, 'What is the kingdom of God like? And to what should I compare it? It is like a mustard seed that someone took and sowed in the garden; it grew and became a tree, and the birds of the air made nests in its branches.'

And again he said, 'To what should I compare the kingdom of God? It is like yeast that a woman took and mixed in with three meaures of flour until all of it was leavened.'

I've always been quite impatient when it comes to planting seeds. The next morning I'll be peering at the soil, expectantly looking for signs of life, and by the third or fourth day I'm convinced that the things are never going to grow. Then, of course, a little while later the first green shoot will appear. Over the following weeks the plants grow bigger and stronger, and my Mum says, 'I told you they would grow'.

So this saying of Jesus makes me think of the need for patience – waiting for the seed to grow into a tree or for the yeast to make the whole batch of dough rise. And I'm reminded of how often we want everything, and we want it now. Even on our Christian journeys we're fond of the dramatic conversion story and the tales of sudden, spectacular changes. While those sorts of accounts are wonderful testimonies to God's goodness, in our rush we can miss what God has been doing in slow, gentle ways in people's lives, or in our own lives. Do I, do you, have the patience to walk alongside people and accompany them as God works in them, over weeks, months and years?

I am convinced that we have a God who is with us for the long haul, and I pray that he will teach me how to be there in the same way for my neighbours.

Loving God, teach me to be patient, and open my eyes to the many ways in which you are at work bringing slow but sure growth in me and in those around me.

Luke 13.22–30

Jesus went through one town and village after another, teaching as he made his way to Jerusalem. Someone asked him, 'Lord, will only a few be saved?' He said to them, 'Strive to enter through the narrow gate; for many, I tell you, will try to enter and will not be able. When once the owner of the house has got up and shut the door, and you begin to stand outside and to knock at the door, saying, "Lord, open to us," then in reply he will say to you, "I do not know where you come from." Then you will begin to say, "We ate and drank with you, and you taught in our streets." But he will say, "I do not know where you come from; go away from me, all you evildoers!" There will be weeping and gnashing of teeth when you see Abraham and Isaac and Jacob and all the prophets in the kingdom of God, and you yourselves thrown out. Then people will come from east and west, from north and south, and will eat in the kingdom of God. Indeed, some are last who will be first, and some are first who will be last.'

'They don't really know me.' Have you ever felt that? I have, yet those I have thought this about have usually known something about me. But most of them would be clueless if asked what made me tick or what I feared. Some have got closer to me, allowing me to share who I am. Even then, although many people know me, few really *know* me. This passage highlights these two types of knowing and the importance of allowing God to *know* us.

Jesus introduces us to people who claimed to know the house-owner on the basis of a casual acquaintance: they had eaten with him and had met with him in the neighbourhood. However, the owner claims not to know where his 'friends' are from (the NIV translates verses 25 and 27 as 'I don't know you, or where you come from'). As a result he does not let them in. The implication of the passage is striking – God (the house-owner) wants to know us in an authentic relationship, one in which the masks disappear and our heart is unveiled and open.

Jesus came to bring us into an intimate relationship with God that transcends the grave and begins in this life. The door is wide open for us to know and be known by God. As we entrust ourselves to him and share our lives with him, we are transformed by him. Yet, as the story warns, the time for us to respond to God is limited. The door will close.

Search me, O God, and know my heart. Test me and know my anxious thoughts; see if there is an offensive way in me and lead me in the way everlasting.

Luke 14.1–6

On one occasion when Jesus was going to the house of a leader of the Pharisees to eat a meal on the sabbath, they were watching him closely. Just then, in front of him, there was a man who had dropsy. And Jesus asked the lawyers and Pharisees, 'Is it lawful to cure people on the sabbath, or not?' But they were silent. So Jesus took him and healed him, and sent him away. Then he said to them, 'If one of you has a child or an ox that has fallen into a well, will you not immediately pull it out on a sabbath day?' And they could not reply to this.

Today's passage follows on from the healing of the crippled woman (Luke 13.10–17). The Pharisees were looking for an opportunity to test Jesus and he met their challenge head on. Jesus cared more about people than about enjoying a meal in comfort and polite conversation.

Why did Jesus ask the question? Of course he was concerned for the crippled man, but he also cared enough for the Pharisees to challenge them over their double standards in applying laws to others that they would not follow themselves.

What difficult questions might Jesus be asking of us at this time? Is it right to ignore those people whom we find most difficult, or those who have problems we would rather ignore? Could Jesus be asking us to represent him in situations that seem to be hopeless, even among groups of people who should know better?

Luke's Gospel doesn't paint the Christian life as easy, but it does show us that in following the way of Christ and serving him faithfully we can find something greater than we could ever hope for. We can bring healing to the sick, hope to the hopeless, and release for those who have become caught up in self-destructive behaviour.

Does the account of Jesus' actions inspire us to reach out to those in need, even in the face of certain opposition? Where might we be called to ask the difficult questions in our world today?

Lord Jesus, help me to be open to your correction. Give me good questions to ask, and the grace and courage to be part of the answer, when appropriate.

Luke 14.7–11

When he noticed how the guests chose the places of honour, he told them a parable: 'When you are invited by some-one to a wedding banquet, do not sit down at the place of honour, in case someone more distinguished than you has been invited by your host; and the host who invited both of you may come and say to you, "Give this person your place", and then in disgrace you would start to take the lowest place. But when you are invited, go and sit down at the lowest place, so that when your host comes, he may say to you, "Friend, move up higher"; then you will be honoured in the presence of all who sit at the table with you. For all who exalt themselves will be humbled, and those who humble themselves will be exalted.'

You need to make a good impression. Ninety-five per cent of what they think of you is determined in the first ten seconds. Well, something like that. Confidence is key. You have to be confident. Otherwise they'll think you're nervous. Nervous and lost. They might start wondering if you're really one of them. That's the last thing you want.

Besides, you deserve to be here so enjoy yourself. Smile. Make the most of the evening. You have a lot to give. It's important that they know that. Get to know the right people. Make sure the right people get to know you.

There's the host. Be confident. And smile.

Now. Where to sit . . .

Who is humble?

The guest who takes the lowest place, who does not fear what others may think, who does not grasp after glory, who waits at the table to hear the host's words, 'Friend, move up higher.'

Who is humble?

The saviour who takes the lowest place, who does not care what others think, who does not grasp after glory, who waits in the tomb to hear the Father's words, 'Son, move up higher.'

Who is humble?

The God who invites us to sit and eat, who does not wait for us to think of him, who shows his glory even in drawing close, who calls to each of us, 'Child, move up higher.'

Heavenly Father, pour your Spirit on us today, that we may follow the example of your Son and learn to live in humility before you and before others.

[49]

Luke 14.12–14

He said also to the one who had invited him, 'When you give a luncheon or a dinner, do not invite your friends or your brothers or your sisters or your relatives or your rich neighbours, in case they might invite you in return, and you would be repaid. But when you give a banquet, invite the poor, the crippled, the lame and the blind. And you will be blessed, because they cannot repay you, for you will be repaid at the resurrection of the righteous.'

This passage talks about the extended family to which we all belong, and the sense of social responsibility that brings, especially to Christians. It also serves to give us a powerful sense of God's grace, for in truth, *we* are the poor, crippled, lame and blind.

We would do well to follow the example Jesus set. He taught us to aid and support the disadvantaged and the socially marginalized; to help outcasts with food, drink, a welcome or clothing. Jesus said, 'Truly I tell you, just as you did it for the least of these who are members of my family, you did it to me' (Matthew 25.40).

Jesus had great compassion for the mentally, spiritually and physically sick, the poor and people who suffered cultural exclusion. He was concerned for all in need of pastoral care, regardless of who they were. For us, those might include members of other faiths or of no faith, and those unattractive, difficult people, who cost us something and give us nothing.

Whoever we are, we are made in the image of our heavenly Father. And we are all equally indebted to him with our lives, because his Son was a sacrifice for all. We are challenged to be ever alert to reflecting Jesus, as best we can, to people we meet. St Teresa of Avila said that Christ has no body on earth but ours. Being his body, we have no choice but to act out of love, not for reward.

Lord Jesus, make our eyes to be like your eyes, and our actions like your actions, so that we may reveal your surprising grace to your world.

Luke 14.25–33

Now large crowds were travelling with him; and he turned and said to them, 'Whoever comes to me and does not hate father and mother, wife and children, brothers and sisters, yes, and even life itself, cannot be my disciple. Whoever does not carry the cross and follow me cannot be my disciple. For which of you, intending to build a tower, does not first sit down and estimate the cost, to see whether he has enough to complete it? Otherwise, when he has laid a foundation and is not able to finish, all who see it will begin to ridicule him, saying, "This fellow began to build and was not able to finish." Or what king, going out to wage war against another king, will not sit down first and consider whether he is able with ten thousand to oppose the one who comes against him with twenty thousand? If he cannot, then, while the other is still far away, he sends a delegation and asks for the terms of peace. So therefore, none of you can become my disciple if you do not give up all your possessions.'

A friend recently suggested to me that his local church was really only interested in 'bums on seats' – pew-fillers boosting the morale of the church leaders and making everyone feel good about being part of a successful church.

Jesus does not seem to be at all impressed by the size of the crowd following him. They had heard the message, seen the miracles, and enjoyed his company, but now it was time to make up their minds. It was easy to join the crowds following Jesus, but much harder to be a disciple. To be his disciple meant to count knowing him as more important than any other relationship or possession, being prepared to sacrifice everything. It was decision time for the crowds. Jesus made it very clear that he was looking for those who were wholeheartedly committed to him.

I was recently travelling in Asia where the cost of commitment is a very real issue for anyone considering turning from Buddhism, Islam or other faiths to follow Christ. Rejecting their birth religion would inevitably mean being rejected by their family and the society in which they grew up. The cost of becoming Jesus' disciple is, for them, massive. Their churches may be small, but very precious to God.

The success of Jesus' mission was not measured by the quantity of his followers but ultimately by his own faithfulness, having counted the cost. Inspired by his perseverance and filled with his Spirit, his disciples went on to be effective apostles. Authentic discipleship today is joining him on a journey that inevitably means loss, but in the long run, a far greater gain.

Lord Jesus, help me to follow you wholeheartedly, having counted the cost.

Luke 15.11–19

Then Jesus said, 'There was a man who had two sons. The younger of them said to his father, "Father, give me the share of the property that will belong to me." So he divided his property between them. A few days later the younger son gathered all he had and travelled to a distant country, and there he squandered his property in dissolute living. When he had spent everything, a severe famine took place throughout that country, and he began to be in need. So he went and hired himself out to one of the citizens of that country, who sent him to his fields to feed the pigs. He would gladly have filled himself with the pods that the pigs were eating; and no one gave him anything. But when he came to himself he said, "How many of my father's hired hands have bread enough and to spare, but here I am dying of hunger! I will get up and go to my father, and I will say to him, 'Father, I have sinned against heaven and before you; I am no longer worthy to be called your son; treat me like one of your hired hands.'"'

For many this episode is well-known and yet today's passage is only half the story and we have to wait for tomorrow's 'happy ending'! Imagine not knowing the outcome and reading, 'to be continued . . .' Having to wait to discover what happens. Living with not knowing the outcome, like the son.

Try and imagine the events and choose one of the characters, father or son. Reread the story, slowly, seeking to put yourself in their shoes and noting your thoughts and feelings.

The father: You've let your son go, given him his inheritance, allowed him to choose. How long has it been since you've seen, or even heard from, him? What do you imagine as you daily think about him? You're in the dark, with no idea how he is, or if you'll see him again. What are your feelings, fears, hopes?

The son: You thought you could have it all, free from the frustrations of home. How are you feeling now – hungry, tired, confused, ill, desperate? What has it taken to come to this decision? Contemplating your life, the journey ahead and your unannounced arrival, what are your feelings, fears, hopes – about yourself and the reception you may receive?

Often we have to live with uncertainty, not knowing the outcome of events, holding our feelings, fears and hopes. Perhaps painfully, lovingly waiting, or making tough decisions in facing our failings, unsure of the repercussions. Take time to draw close to our loving God, who holds us in the palm of his hand, and is our source of comfort even as we live with uncertainty (2 Corinthians 1.3–5).

Lord, when we or our loved ones stray into 'a distant country', give us grace to come to our senses and to return to you.

Luke 15.20–24

'So he set off and went to his father. But while he was still far off, his father saw him and was filled with compassion; he ran and put his arms around him and kissed him. Then the son said to him, "Father, I have sinned against heaven and before you; I am no longer worthy to be called your son." But the father said to his slaves, "Quickly, bring out a robe – the best one – and put it on him; put a ring on his finger and sandals on his feet. And get the fatted calf and kill it, and let us eat and celebrate; for this son of mine was dead and is alive again; he was lost and is found!" And they began to celebrate.'

An extremely burly man once sat in front of me on the bus. He looked like a 'Hell's Angel', complete with pierced eyebrow, bald head, beard, black T-shirt and studded leather jacket. He did not sit alone. Alongside him sat his pretty little daughter. I did not expect this burly man to show the devoted, fatherly love I witnessed during that journey. They happily chatted together, him proudly smiling down at her as she snuggled up to him. In the same way, this passage touches our hearts deeply because the love that the father shows surprises us and fills us with hope.

Yet, this passage should not just warm our hearts; it challenges our actions. There was a little girl called Nidu in the crèche I worked at in India. To get a reaction from me Nidu would slap me, pull my hair, pinch me and generally misbehave. I could have responded with anger. And initially I did. However, as Christians loved by our heavenly father we are challenged not only to feel God's love, but also to emulate his love to others. So, every time Nidu would pull my hair I'd grab her hand and kiss it, and every time she'd slap me I'd pull her into my lap and cuddle her. The effect of my love for her changed her. Nidu became a docile and affectionate little girl.

That is the challenge of this passage to us. As we experience God's love we are to reflect that love to those around us, so that they may feel that love and pass it on, like a Chinese whisper that never ends.

Father God, thank you for your unconditional love, and for those parents, family and friends who have cared for us and shown us glimpses of that love in this world.

Luke 15.25–32

'Now his elder brother was in the field; and when he came and approached the house, he heard music and dancing. He called one of the slaves and asked what was going on. He replied, "Your brother has come, and your father has killed the fatted calf, because he has come back safe and sound." Then he became angry and refused to go in. His father came out and began to plead with him. But he answered his father, "Listen! For all these years I have been working like a slave for you, and I have never disobeyed your command; yet you have never given me even a young goat so that I might celebrate with my friends. But when this son of yours came back, who has devoured your property with prostitutes, you killed the fatted calf for him!" Then the father said to him, "Son, you are always with me, and all that is mine is yours. But we had to celebrate and rejoice, because this brother of yours was dead and has come to life; he was lost and has been found."'

I am blessed with a large family. When we get together it's a very special occasion, and there is always a party! On such occasions, it's not unusual for there to be someone who remains outside, feeling angry, jealous, upset, or simply feeling left out. And invariably, one family member or another will go out to plead with them to come back in, 'Don't spoil the party.' It reminds me of the elder brother in the story of the prodigal son.

Whenever this Bible passage is read, a very good Christian friend of mine always says she can't help empathizing with the elder brother. The good son, the one who stayed at home, worked hard and never gave his father any trouble while his wayward brother wasted his inheritance and got into all sorts of scrapes. Yet the party was given for him! We may recognise in ourselves the dubious qualities of anger, resentment and jealousy that we see in the elder brother.

The good news is that the father leaves the party. He gets up from the top table in full view of all his guests, and he goes out in search of his elder son. He pleads with him to come inside and join the celebrations. We are not told how the elder son responded. But surely this passage teaches us more than how difficult it can be sometimes to rejoice with those who rejoice (Romans 12.15). Our heavenly Father is eager for us to join the party and not stay outside playing comparison games in bitter frustration about what is fair and what's not. Two sons in this parable are welcomed home, but the welcome must be received.

Lord, grant us forgiving hearts that take the initiative to welcome home whomever you bring back to your family.

Luke 16.10–13

'Whoever is faithful in a very little is faithful also in much; and whoever is dishonest in a very little is dishonest also in much. If then you have not been faithful with the dishonest wealth, who will entrust to you the true riches? And if you have not been faithful with what belongs to another, who will give you what is your own? No slave can serve two masters; for a slave will either hate the one and love the other, or be devoted to the one and despise the other. You cannot serve God and wealth.'

The comedian Groucho Marx was once asked how to tell if a man was honest. 'There's one way to find out,' Marx replied. 'Ask him. If he says, "Yes", you know he's a crook.'

Unlike the temperature, faithfulness and honesty are not counted in degrees.

We can either be trusted, or we can't. We see the proof in all areas of life. When we are in trouble we are more likely to seek out the friend who keeps our confidences than the one who just can't keep a secret. In the business world, the person who can be trusted in a very small thing may well be promoted to far greater responsibilities. It's the way that individuals climb to the top. On the flipside, those who embezzle large sums probably began with much smaller amounts and little acts of dishonesty, things we see as too small to matter.

God does not judge us by the extent of an act, whether generous or greedy, but rather by the motives which form and shape it. A small action can reflect who we really are quite as easily as a large one.

Driving every decision and action is our core belief, not only who we are but *whose* we are. 'No servant can serve two masters.' We can only wear the colours of one team. Who do you answer to?

Lord, help me to live in integrity, proving in the little things as well as in the large that I belong to you.

Luke 16.19–31

'There was a rich man who was dressed in purple and fine linen and who feasted sumptuously every day. And at his gate lay a poor man named Lazarus, covered in sores, who longed to satisfy his hunger with what fell from the rich man's table; even the dogs would come and lick his sores. The poor man died and was carried away by the angels to be with Abraham. The rich man also died and was buried. In Hades, where he was being tormented, he looked up and saw Abraham far away with Lazarus by his side. He called out, "Father Abraham, have mercy on me, and send Lazarus to dip the tip of his finger in water and cool my tongue; for I am in agony in these flames." But Abraham said, "Child, remember that during your lifetime you received your good things, and Lazarus in like manner evil things; but now he is comforted here, and you are in agony. Besides all this, between you and us a chasm has been fixed, so that those who might want to pass from here to you cannot do so, and no one can cross from there to us." He said, "Then, father, I beg you to send him to my father's house – for I have five brothers – that he may warn them, so that they will not also come into this place of torment." Abraham replied, "They have Moses and the prophets; they should listen to them." He said, "No, father Abraham; but if someone goes to them from the dead, they will repent." He said to him, "If they do not listen to Moses and the prophets, neither will they be convinced even if someone rises from the dead."'

This passage is a rich picking-ground for the sort of theological controversy beloved by many in the church. It has fed endless debate on the nature of heaven and hell, some of which, of course, is useful and necessary, and on the afterlife in general.

However, as more than one wise sage has said, 'It is not the bits of the Bible I don't understand that give me the most trouble – it's the bits I *do* understand!' We have enough to be getting on with in putting into practice what we *do* know of our Lord Jesus Christ and the life he wants us to live in following him.

Jesus' challenge to the Pharisees here is just that: to get on with what they already know of God in 'Moses and the prophets' – without that first basic step, they'll hardly be convinced by someone rising 'from the dead'. It's hard not to hear in this tale echoes of Jesus' actual raising of another Lazarus (in John's Gospel). And sure enough, those who weren't interested in following Jesus weren't much impressed by that amazing event, either. There is also a looking-forward, here, to the end of the story, to Jesus' own resurrection from the dead.

As we follow what we know of Jesus, however much or little we feel that might be, he'll lead us through the next part of the story – through the darkness of the cross and out into the light of a deeper understanding of the new life he shares with us in his resurrection.

Lord Jesus, help me to follow you in what I do know, and so lead me into a deeper knowing.

Luke 17.1–4

Jesus said to his disciples, 'Occasions for stumbling are bound to come, but woe to anyone by whom they come! It would be better for you if a millstone were hung around your neck and you were thrown into the sea than for you to cause one of these little ones to stumble. Be on your guard! If another disciple sins, you must rebuke the offender, and if there is repentance, you must forgive. And if the same person sins against you seven times a day, and turns back to you seven times and says, "I repent", you must forgive.'

Tired and stressed people can react badly to injustices, and patience wears thin with repeated offence. Tired and stressed managers get angry when instructions are not followed, particularly after special efforts to make them clear. Tired and stressed parents feel completely justified in getting cross with disobedient children.

Just *occasionally* my child takes too long to respond obediently. When for the third or fourth time I have asked for compliance or an end to misbehaviour, I observe a pattern: the volume increases, I get cross, and there may be warnings and sanctions imposed for taking no notice.

I justify my reaction, and feel indignant at disobedience. The result is sometimes a nasty and noisy mess.

Reading this passage turns the magnifying glass not on the perpetrator of the wrong but on the one who is wronged, or disobeyed, or who suffers an injustice. On me.

Jesus values repentance far higher than any feelings of self-righteousness that I might feel. He is saying, 'At the slightest hint of an apology, rush in with forgiveness, and reward it highly. Reinforce that attitude, and show that it pays to be sorry.' Only that way can there be change, and only that way is there any point in changing.

If we do not forgive, the battle lines become fixed and hardened; we become a stumbling block to the little one. The only way forward is to forgive.

Lord, grant me patience. Help me to value repentance in others, so that I may more fully appreciate your daily forgiveness of me.

Luke 17.11–19

On the way to Jerusalem Jesus was going through the region between Samaria and Galilee. As he entered a village, ten lepers approached him. Keeping their distance, they called out, saying, 'Jesus, Master, have mercy on us!' When he saw them, he said to them, 'Go and show yourselves to the priests.' And as they went, they were made clean. Then one of them, when he saw that he was healed, turned back, praising God with a loud voice. He prostrated himself at Jesus' feet and thanked him. And he was a Samaritan. Then Jesus asked, 'Were not ten made clean? But the other nine, where are they? Was none of them found to return and give praise to God except this foreigner?' Then he said to him, 'Get up and go on your way; your faith has made you well.'

It may sound obvious but in this story there seems to be a connection between the leper's dependency on Jesus and his level of gratitude.

Lepers were dependent on others for their well-being, as they had no land or livestock of their own. When a *rabbi* (teacher), or anyone for that matter, walked by it was natural to ask for help. Jesus had compassion and healed all ten lepers but only one, the one who wasn't even a Jew, came back with an overflowing 'Thank you'. We don't know what happened to the other nine but for this leper the healing seemed to be more than just skin deep.

When I read the story I felt deeply inadequate, realizing that my level of gratitude to Jesus is very shallow. We can get on with life, feeling that we can get by on our own. But stories like these can lead us to a different way of living, a way of living where *gratefulness* becomes a habit – because gratefulness is an acknowledgment of our dependency on God. It's an act of faith.

This story invites us to think about how dependent we really are on Jesus. But perhaps we should also be asking 'How grateful am I?' Meister Eckhart said 'If the only prayer you ever say in your entire life is "Thank you", it will be enough.' May we be like the one leper and realize how totally dependent we are on Jesus, overflowing with thanks to him.

Heavenly Father, thank you. Teach me to be grateful every day of my life.

Luke 17.20–25

Once Jesus was asked by the Pharisees when the kingdom of God was coming, and he answered, 'The kingdom of God is not coming with things that can be observed; nor will they say, "Look, here it is!" or "There it is!" For, in fact, the kingdom of God is among you.'

Then he said to the disciples, 'The days are coming when you will long to see one of the days of the Son of Man, and you will not see it. They will say to you, "Look there!" or "Look here!" Do not go, do not set off in pursuit. For as the lightning flashes and lights up the sky from one side to the other, so will the Son of Man be in his day. But first he must endure much suffering and be rejected by this generation.'

I lived for several years in a country that ranks among the five most corrupt in the world. Corruption is a poison: it means potholed roads and dysfunctional social services, suffocated businesses and apathetic people – all punctuated by the few who drive by, oblivious, in BMWs. The worst victims often remain invisible, like the uneducated, unsupervized, and mostly forgotten orphans in soulless institutions that make visitors gag or weep.

Often, leaving an orphanage, I prayed, 'When is the kingdom of God coming? When will You fix this broken world?' The Pharisees asked the same question, because the prophets of old had promised hope to our corrupt world: someday God would bring life and justice by sending his Messiah, the good king who cares about orphans and promises to establish a kingdom of his own.

But when?

'The kingdom of God is among you,' Jesus replied; for he was the king, and he brought the kingdom wherever he went. He came not with trumpets and armies – 'Look, here it is!' – but with words of love and his death on a cross. The cross is the hope of the hopeless, for it brought to nothing the power of injustice. Its victim, Jesus, rose from the dead, undaunted, and assured his followers that one day he would return and make things right.

But for now, 'the kingdom of God is among you'. Among his followers, the world gets a preview of the kingdom: within our communities as we love one another, without as we bring God's justice and truth to the world. We taste, and the world sees, what good news the kingdom of God is.

Your kingdom come,
Your will be done,
On earth as in heaven.

Luke 18.9–14

He also told this parable to some who trusted in themselves that they were righteous and regarded others with contempt: 'Two men went up to the temple to pray, one a Pharisee and the other a tax collector. The Pharisee, standing by himself, was praying thus, "God, I thank you that I am not like other people: thieves, rogues, adulterers, or even like this tax collector. I fast twice a week; I give a tenth of all my income." But the tax collector, standing far off, would not even look up to heaven, but was beating his breast and saying, "God, be merciful to me, a sinner!" I tell you, this man went down to his home justified rather than the other; for all who exalt themselves will be humbled, but all who humble themselves will be exalted.'

I have become increasingly aware of how quick I am to pass judgement on others. As I walk through the streets I make assumptions about those I see around me: the homeless tramp getting drunk, the smartly dressed business man rudely pushing his way along the pavement, the hooded-top-clad teenagers wandering around in large groups. I perceive myself to be a better citizen than them and feel good about myself.

In the same way I make judgements about those in church. I have been fortunate to attend churches with congregations representing the whole mix of society. But I notice when someone turns up late for the service, or stumbles over a reading, or passes on the collection plate without putting anything in. The fact that I notice these things betrays my own sense of superiority. And this parable is aimed at people like me.

Jesus is reminding us that we cannot earn our approval before God. When we become proud of our gifts, and focus on what we are doing for God, then we miss the point. We should not regard others with contempt but see each person as a beloved creation of God. That should instil a desire to reach out to the outcasts rather than exclude them. And, as we spend time helping those around us rather than judging them, we will become more like the tax collector – humble before God and society.

Heavenly Father, lead us in the way of humility. Grant us grace to recognize our own faults and to value others more highly than ourselves.

Luke 18.15–17

People were bringing even infants to him that he might touch them; and when the disciples saw it, they sternly ordered them not to do it. But Jesus called for them and said, 'Let the little children come to me, and do not stop them; for it is to such as these that the kingdom of God belongs. Truly I tell you, whoever does not receive the kingdom of God as a little child will never enter it.'

I have a young daughter, a toddler, with whom I have recently started to pray. I used to pray for her quietly as she drank her evening bottle of milk before going to sleep. Limited as her understanding and vocabulary may be, now we pray together.

Each night I ask her if she wants to pray. She always agrees and so I pray that the Lord will be with her, that he will bless her and help her to grow in her body, her mind, her emotions and her spirit. I say 'Amen' and, with her thumb or the bottle between her lips, she whispers 'Amen' from the corner of her mouth.

Each day without fail, she thinks for a moment and then looks up to me and says 'More?'

Smiling, I say 'OK' and, before I can suggest anything, she knows who is next – 'Mummy?' So we pray for Mummy together. Once again, she says 'Amen', pauses and again asks for 'More?' Daddy is next, then her brother, her grandparents and sometimes others that she has met that day.

She doesn't yet have the words to pray herself, but she readily agrees with my prayers and always prompts me to pray a little 'more'.

When I come to prayer and struggle to find words that express my heart to God, I forget that all I really need to do is look to my daughter and be like a 'little child'. What could express our hearts better than to look up into the eyes of our great High Priest who 'always lives to make intercession' for us and ask him simply for 'More?'

Lord Jesus Christ, you are ready to do more than we ask or imagine; give us this day a new confidence when we pray in your name.

Luke 18.18–27

A certain ruler asked him, 'Good Teacher, what must I do to inherit eternal life?' Jesus said to him, 'Why do you call me good? No one is good but God alone. You know the commandments: "You shall not commit adultery; You shall not murder; You shall not steal; You shall not bear false witness; Honour your father and mother."' He replied, 'I have kept all these since my youth.' When Jesus heard this, he said to him, 'There is still one thing lacking. Sell all that you own and distribute the money to the poor, and you will have treasure in heaven; then come, follow me.' But when he heard this, he became sad; for he was very rich. Jesus looked at him and said, 'How hard it is for those who have wealth to enter the kingdom of God! Indeed, it is easier for a camel to go through the eye of a needle than for someone who is rich to enter the kingdom of God.'

Those who heard it said, 'Then who can be saved?' He replied, 'What is impossible for mortals is possible for God.'

A few years ago, Adidas ran an advertising campaign with the slogan 'Impossible Is Nothing'. They were suggesting that with the right equipment, and the right amount of personal dedication, we could accomplish our wildest sporting fantasies. The myth of human progress claims that with the correct technological equipment there is no limitation on human possibilities.

Yet the rich ruler who encounters Jesus is confronted by a stark appraisal of human limitations. Despite his virtuous obedience, his riches will prevent him from entering God's kingdom. This apparently simple teaching story about the necessity of relinquishing wealth has a deep message for us.

The rich man is offered treasure in heaven, yet prefers his wealth on earth. Two kingdoms battle for his allegiance. The conflict between the two is at the heart of Jesus' message. The kingdom of heaven is near, and will displace the kingdoms of this world. Jesus calls us to repent, and give our allegiance to God's rule. We, like the rich ruler, are caught in the in-between times. We know that by Christ's death and resurrection, the powers of this age (sin and death) are defeated, and that the rule of Christ's risen life has begun. Yet like the rich ruler, we still live with the misplaced desires for the comforts of this present age.

It is easy to buy into the myth of human progress, to try to 'save ourselves'. But when confronted with Christ's personal call on our lives, in whatever form, we feel overwhelmed by the apparent impossibility of following faithfully. That is when we need to remember that 'what is impossible for mortals is possible for God'.

Lord, help us to hear your call to relinquish all for the sake of the kingdom, and to hear your promise that what is impossible for us is possible for you.

Luke 18.28–34

Then Peter said, 'Look, we have left our homes and followed you.' And he said to them, 'Truly I tell you, there is no one who has left house or wife or brothers or parents or children, for the sake of the kingdom of God, who will not get back very much more in this age, and in the age to come eternal life.'

Then he took the twelve aside and said to them, 'See, we are going up to Jerusalem, and everything that is written about the Son of God by the prophets will be accomplished. For he will be handed over to the Gentiles; and he will be mocked and insulted and spat upon. After they have flogged him, they will kill him, and on the third day he will rise again.' But they understood nothing about these things; in fact, what he said was hidden from them, and they did not grasp what was said.

I started leading the High Level group of walking guests up the slopes of Garbh Bheinn, in Ardgour near Glen Coe. Like most Scottish mountains, it rises steeply and unrelentingly from near sea-level to the summit. I picked a route along terraces up the side of a ravine, and we ascended into the mist as we climbed. At about 2,200 feet up, the ground levelled out and we were in a nondescript area of hillocks and tarns. It was darker, wet and the mist had become a fog. However, I had been up there several times before, and had the map, route description and my compass. We made the summit cairn but it was clear given the worsening weather that my priority was now to get the party down the hill quickly.

Using the map and compass to check the route, I started descending the northeast flank. Visibility was about 20 metres and the rain was in our faces. But after a few minutes the ground and the route on the map didn't correspond. Eventually I found a novel way down a ravine with spectacular mountain scenery that few people have seen.

My party trusted me to lead them. We didn't know when we started that we would have a difficult, even dangerous, day. But throughout they kept trusting their leader. That was the last week I led, partly because my confidence was dented by that experience.

The disciples left everything and followed their leader. Jesus knew where the journey would lead but kept walking. They trusted him, and he gave them – gives us – much more than spectacular scenery.

Lord Jesus, help us to keep following you, trusting in your promise of eternal life.

Luke 19.1–10

He entered Jericho and was passing through it. A man was there named Zacchaeus; he was a chief tax-collector and was rich. He was trying to see who Jesus was, but on account of the crowd he could not, because he was short in stature. So he ran ahead and climbed a sycamore tree to see him, because he was going to pass that way. When Jesus came to the place, he looked up and said to him, 'Zacchaeus, hurry and come down; for I must stay at your house today.' So he hurried down and was happy to welcome him. All who saw it began to grumble and said, 'He has gone to be the guest of one who is a sinner.' Zacchaeus stood there and said to the Lord, 'Look, half of my possessions, Lord, I will give to the poor; and if I have defrauded anyone of anything, I will pay back four times as much.' Then Jesus said to him, 'Today salvation has come to this house, because he too is a son of Abraham. For the Son of Man came to seek out and to save the lost.'

Of the many heroes and villains in the Bible, some of the most memorable are described with particular reference to a physical feature or attribute. Elijah was hairy, Samson had tremendous strength, and Zacchaeus? Zacchaeus was short.

For a man whose occupation saw him bracketed together with prostitutes and sinners, his parents had a remarkable lack of foresight. They must have had no inkling of his future career path when they gave him a name that comes from the Greek for 'pure'. But everyone would have known that the wealth of this man, who was not just a tax collector but the head honcho, came from squirreling away a percentage of their hard-earned cash. The irony of his name would not have been lost on the first-century inhabitants of Jericho.

As the crowd gathered, it was not just his lack of height that meant he was unable to see. A popular man would have been allowed to push through to the front for a better view, but not Zacchaeus. His tenacity made sure he got more than the glimpse of Jesus he might have hoped for. The risk he took (climbing a tree made him a ready target!) paid off. He could never have imagined that Jesus wanted to meet and eat with him, or that his own values would be transformed in a few moments.

Curiosity may have 'killed the cat', but for Zaccheus it led to new life.

Lord, as the one who wants us to sit and eat at your banqueting table, give us the curiosity and strength for a clearer vision of you.

Luke 19.29–40

When he had come near Bethphage and Bethany, at the place called the Mount of Olives, he sent two of the disciples, saying, 'Go into the village ahead of you, and as you enter it you will find tied there a colt that has never been ridden. Untie it and bring it here. If anyone asks you, "Why are you untying it?" just say this: "The Lord needs it."' So those who were sent departed and found it as he had told them. As they were untying the colt, its owners asked them, 'Why are you untying the colt?' They said, 'The Lord needs it.' Then they brought it to Jesus; and after throwing their cloaks on the colt, they set Jesus on it. As he rode along, people kept spreading their cloaks on the road. As he was now approaching the path down from the Mount of Olives, the whole multitude of the disciples began to praise God joyfully with a loud voice for all the deeds of power that they had seen, saying,

> Blessed is the king
> who comes in the name of the Lord!
> Peace in heaven,
> and glory in the highest heaven!

Some of the Pharisees in the crowd said to him, 'Teacher, order your disciples to stop.' He answered 'I tell you, if these were silent, the stones would shout out.'

Trekking a short section of an ancient trade route in Nepal last October, I had numerous opportunities to observe the donkeys. Carrying saddle packs of rice, Budweiser boxes stuffed with apples, and cages of red squawking chickens, they patiently suffered a variety of indignities. Forced to teeter across torrential rivers on rocking steel bridges, picking their way up and down steep flights of rock-hewn steps, and frequently on the receiving end of the impassive driver's whip, they unfailingly put one foot in front of another, occasionally taking pause to find the right step, but always making forward progress.

Their eyes were soft, their heads down, their ears up. We, the tourist trekkers, pressed into the rock face as the long trains went by. Someone told a story of the tourist who had grown livid at the donkeys for spoiling his trek, and in a fit of rage had pushed one over the cliff edge into the white water below.

As I read the Palm Sunday account recently, it was hard not to see the donkey as more than a symbol of Jesus' humility and his peaceful kingdom. In biblical times, too, the donkey was a means of transport across difficult terrain. Five days after the procession into Jerusalem, like beasts of burden then and now, Jesus would make his own resolute progress under the driver's whip, bearing the burden of our pain, frustration, anger, fear, grief, and rebellion. On Palm Sunday the unspoilt young male donkey carries the king into Jerusalem; on Good Friday the unspoilt young male king would carry the sin of the world to the cross.

Lord Jesus, may my life also show the qualities of humility, patience and resolve that you displayed during the last week of your life on earth.

Luke 19.45–48

Then he entered the temple and began to drive out those who were selling things there; and he said,

It is written,
'My house shall be a house of prayer';
But you have made it a den of robbers.

Every day he was teaching in the temple. The chief priests, the scribes, and the leaders of the people kept looking for a way to kill him; but they did not find anything they could do, for all the people were spellbound by what they heard.

The opening scenes of the film *Saving Private Ryan* graphically depict the early days of the retaking of occupied France from the hands of the German army in 1944. If you've seen it, you won't have forgotten the scenes of devastation on the Normandy beaches. Some of the most dramatic stories of the Second World War involve the retaking of land – often islands like Crete and Sicily – held by the invader. There was almost a collective sigh of relief from the rightful inhabitants when the fighting was over and land and institutions were put back in the hands of the people to whom they belonged.

In one way Jesus' whole life was a kind of invasion – a bridgehead – into a world occupied by a foreign power. So in this passage he storms the temple and takes it back from the people who have occupied it and exploited it for their own purposes of money-making, social control and religious oppression.

While he was still a child, Jesus acted as if the temple were his home; it was where his Father lived (Luke 2.49). In the day after his entry into Jerusalem he first clears it of everyone and everything that stops it from being a house of prayer. Then he shows his sense of belonging and rightful ownership by taking centre stage and preaching his own gospel right in front of the powerful elite who wish him dead. His courage and authority are breathtaking. There is no doubt who is in command here.

Lord Jesus, I worship you today because you command the heavens and the earth. Be in command of my life, and clear it so that it can be full of prayer and a temple to your Father's glory.

Luke 20.45–21.4

In the hearing of all the people he said to the disciples, 'Beware of the scribes, who like to walk around in long robes, and love to be greeted with respect in the market-places, and to have the best seats in the synagogues and places of honour at banquets. They devour widows' houses and for the sake of appearance say long prayers. They will receive the greater condemnation.'

He looked up and saw rich people putting their gifts into the treasury; he also saw a poor widow put in two small copper coins. He said, 'Truly I tell you, this poor widow has put in more than all of them; for all of them have contributed out of their abundance, but she out of her poverty has put in all she had to live on.'

'In the hearing of all . . .' What must it have been like to be a disciple? Never quite being sure whom Jesus was watching and what he was going to say next — often so painfully in public. I can hear them sucking in their breath and wincing as the heads of people turned in Jesus' direction and others stormed towards him, defending themselves. Jesus' words could be surgically incisive and penetrating, yet at the same time mysterious and tender.

In this instance he saw through the crowds of wealthy worshippers to the widow. God doesn't appear to be good at sums. The widow obviously hadn't 'put in more than all of them'. But Jesus lives according to a different kind of economy than our own. The characteristics and qualities of the kingdom rule of God are upside down, counter-cultural, even absurd to many.

Jesus' life and teachings draw back the veil on a revolutionary way: the paradox of an itinerant King of Glory — the creator God — with no place to lay his head. One man, obedient to death so that all people and all creation might live. His ministry and kingdom deeply challenged and offended sensibilities, but also revealed a seemingly reckless mercy, a profligate grace and an extravagant love.

God's economics may seem faulty and his justice somehow impenetrable, but even today his eyes search among the crowd and watch for our response to his initiative.

Lord Jesus, help me to live today a life that is pleasing in your sight — according to your values, in the light of your life and in response to your grace.

Luke 21.37–22.6

Every day he was teaching in the temple, and at night he would go out and spend the night on the Mount of Olives, as it was called. And all the people would get up early in the morning to listen to him in the temple.

Now the festival of Unleavened Bread, which is called the Passover, was near.

The chief priests and the scribes were looking for a way to put Jesus to death, for they were afraid of the people. Then Satan entered into Judas called Iscariot, who was one of the twelve; he went away and conferred with the chief priests and officers of the temple police about how he might betray him to them. They were greatly pleased and agreed to give him money. So he consented and began to look for an opportunity to betray him to them when no crowd was present.

The sense of urgency increases. Jesus teaches every day, the people even arriving early to hear him. The chief priests and scribes are looking hard for a way to kill him. The tension increases for us too, as Maundy Thursday and Good Friday approach and we come to the horror of those last days of the journey to the cross.

Judas' motive is uncertain but clearly this isn't simply a moment of weakness, a betrayal under pressure. It is a premeditated and planned act.

We either love to hate Judas or we feel sorry for him. After all, wasn't Jesus' death part of God's saving plan? But Judas also makes us feel uncomfortable. Surely we could never be like him . . . could we?

Judas wasn't a monster. He may have been a bit fond of money but it certainly wasn't obvious to the other disciples that he was a betrayer. 'Who would do such a thing?'

The question for us is 'How different are we?' How often, perhaps out of disappointment, do we betray Jesus with a word, an omission, an action or a thought? It is not difficult to condemn and accuse. We underestimate the implications of our actions. Perhaps Judas did too.

Despite the pain and sadness of the next few days we have assurance that through the death of Christ we are forgiven, and that we can be changed. But as we enter into the coming bleakness we do well to ponder how we respond to disappointment, as we discover afresh the greatness of what Christ has done for us.

Lord Jesus, save us from all that threatens to draw us away from you. Give us courage and strength to remain faithful to you even in the times of hardship and great trial.

Luke 22.39–46

He came out and went, as was his custom, to the Mount of Olives; and the disciples followed him. When he reached the place, he said to them, 'Pray that you may not come into the time of trial.' Then he withdrew from them about a stone's throw, knelt down, and prayed, 'Father, if you are willing, remove this cup from me; yet, not my will but yours be done.' Then an angel from heaven appeared to him and gave him strength. In his anguish he prayed more earnestly, and his sweat became like great drops of blood falling down on the ground. When he got up from prayer, he came to the disciples and found them sleeping because of grief, and he said to them, 'Why are you sleeping? Get up and pray that you may not come into the time of trial.'

DAY 44 – WEEK 7 – MAUNDY THURSDAY

Someone once said, 'Don't pray for lighter burdens, but for stronger backs.' The truth of that saying is born out in today's reading. Jesus knew he was facing an ordeal of unimaginable agony, both physical and spiritual. His anguish was plain to see and it brought him to his knees.

If we had been in Jesus' place, what would we have prayed?

'Lord, give me a way out.'

'God, why are you letting this happen to me?'

Well, the good news is that it's perfectly human to react to horrible situations like that. Even Jesus prayed, 'remove this cup from me'. Yet, though God is a God of miracles, the blessings we're most likely to receive in times of trial are his tangible presence with us, his peace in spite of circumstances, and his strength for the road ahead. Trusting in his Father's love, Jesus was eventually able to pray, 'not my will but yours be done'.

This lesson is one I'm learning the hard way. A year ago I fell ill with a mystery illness. In the absence of any firm diagnosis my mind began to fill in the blanks with worse case scenarios. For three months I lived in constant fear: fear of the unknown, fear of my own mortality. Despite the faithful prayers of my family and friends, God didn't take the illness away. What, gradually, he did take was the fear, and left in its place his peace and strength. For the first time in my life I really began to understand what it meant to call God, 'my refuge and my fortress' (Psalm 91.2).

Lord, thank you for your faithfulness. Whatever I face in life, teach me to pray with the psalmist, 'my refuge and my fortress; my God, in whom I trust'.

Luke 23.32–38

Two others also, who were criminals, were led away to be put to death with him. When they came to the place that is called The Skull, they crucified Jesus there with the criminals, one on his right and one on his left. Then Jesus said, 'Father, forgive them; for they do not know what they are doing.' And they cast lots to divide his clothing. And the people stood by, watching; but the leaders scoffed at him, saying, 'He saved others; let him save himself if he is the Messiah of God, his chosen one!' The soldiers also mocked him, coming up and offering him sour wine, and saying, 'If you are the King of the Jews, save yourself!' There was also an inscription over him, 'This is the King of the Jews.'

To the bystander, the death of Jesus must have looked like a complete failure. For the Christian, the cross is at the very heart of the gospel message and is the greatest victory the world has ever seen.

Jesus is crucified surrounded by insults, yet as he dies he is still thinking of others. 'Father, forgive them, for they do not know what they are doing.' Luke does not dwell on the physical pain of the crucifixion. Instead he draws us to the fulfilment of scripture (Psalm 22.6–8) by alluding to the cruel mocking voices of the people who stand watching as Jesus dies and shout, 'He saved others, let him save himself.' But the people did not know that the Chosen One, the saviour of the world must suffer and die, as Isaiah 53.5 (NIV) says:

> But he was pierced for our transgressions, he was crushed for our iniquities; the punishment that brought us peace was upon him, and by his wounds we are healed.

The irony is obvious. If Jesus had taken the advice of the people and 'saved himself' he would not have saved anyone. He selflessly gave his life for us to bring everyone freedom, when no one present recognized what was really happening. They truly did not know what they were doing, as he poured himself out for them and for us. What depths of love this is, to absorb all the evil that humanity could throw at him without giving it back in return. The sign above his bleeding head read, 'This is the King of the Jews.' Today give thanks in your heart that the king died for you!

Lord Jesus, thank you for your most wonderful act of love, your gift to the world.

Luke 23.50–56

Now there was a good and righteous man named Joseph, who, though a member of the council, had not agreed to their plan and action. He came from the Jewish town of Arimathea, and he was waiting expectantly for the kingdom of God. This man went to Pilate and asked for the body of Jesus. Then he took it down, wrapped it in a linen cloth, and laid it in a rock-hewn tomb where no one had ever been laid. It was the day of Preparation, and the sabbath was beginning. The women who had come with him from Galilee followed, and they saw the tomb and how his body was laid. Then they returned, and prepared spices and ointments.

On the sabbath they rested according to the commandment.

Dead. Not just extinguished but extinct. Dreams like autumn leaves skittering across the grass, piling up in corners, mouldering. Unseen, unknown, unrealized. So much venom and hatred, *within* the household of God!

He was light and love. Joy and hope. Peace and gentleness. Laughter and lightness of spirit. Warmth. A quick answer; a quirky retort, phenomenal wisdom. Grace. Truth. Love. Unconditional, abundant, rapturous and stunning . . . love!

Beaten, bloodied . . . buried.

How long was that day? A mere twenty-four hours? Gut-wrenching, nauseating, endless, screaming, inescapable hours of inconsolable anguish?

The Love-Of-My-Life – gone. My Dad – gone. My babies – gone. My best friend, my mother, brother, sister, my lover . . . hope, dreams, future. Gone.

The scents of myrrh and frankincense; suffering and sorrow. Here we sit, waiting. Waiting for the agonizing hours to pass. Waiting for the waves of piercing pain to release our wrung-out hearts. Waiting for the faintest glimmer of a day worth waking up for.

Sitting in the darkest, loneliest, most harrowing place on earth, where our only acquaintance is grief that will not let us go.

Here we sit. Waiting. Utterly, unspeakably, desolate.

Dear Lord, help us to trust you when we sit in desolation. Help us to come back to you on our Easter Saturdays, even when we cannot see that you are at work in the dark, redeeming and resurrecting all that we surrender to you.

Luke 24.1–12

But on the first day of the week, at early dawn, they came to the tomb, taking the spices that they had prepared. They found the stone rolled away from the tomb, but when they went in, they did not find the body. While they were perplexed about this, suddenly two men in dazzling clothes stood beside them. The women were terrified and bowed their faces to the ground, but the men said to them, 'Why do you look for the living among the dead? He is not here, but has risen. Remember how he told you, while he was still in Galilee, that the Son of Man must be handed over to sinners, and be crucified, and on the third day rise again.' Then they remembered his words, and returning from the tomb, they told all this to the eleven and to all the rest. Now it was Mary Magdalene, Joanna, Mary the mother of James, and the other women with them who told this to the apostles. But these words seemed to them an idle tale, and they did not believe them. But Peter got up and ran to the tomb; stooping and looking in, he saw the linen cloths by themselves; then he went home, amazed at what had happened.

In the words of the song 'And so the journey ends . . .', or does it? For the women who walked to the tomb that first Easter Sunday, this was their expectation. Loss, dejection, bewilderment – but the story of their lives was about to be turned upside down and transformed. First, there was no stone to move. Next, there was no body. Luke's recording of this event, 'While they were perplexed about this . . .' probably wins the prize in the whole of his Gospel for understatement! Then, they meet two angels. Have you ever been on a journey where the unexpected happens?

But the journey was not only unexpected. The women also realize that they are lost and are looking in the wrong place. Then, in the words of another song, they have one of those 'It's all coming back to me now' moments. What did Jesus say? On the third day, he will rise again. Now, the reality of his words hit home and they have one of those 'the truth will set you free moments' or, rather, 'The Truth will set you free'.

The journey of Jesus this first Easter Sunday morning is open-ended, opening up a way beyond the cross and into resurrection. It is his story and it is now our turn to tell our world of who he is and what he has done. Of course, there will be some, perhaps many, who don't believe. But there will be others like Peter who will look into it further, and find themselves 'amazed'.

Father God, on this glorious day, give us opportunities to tell the story of the risen Christ to your world.

The Contributors

Matt Coles, Simon Elliott, David Green, Mary Hancock, Mark Harris, Jeremy Haswell, Simon Heron, Richard Higginson, James Hill, Tina Hodgett, Alison Hogger, Clive Hogger, Craig Holmes, Jane Holmes, Tim Horlock, Ian Hughes, Graham Hunter, Lisa Jackson, Mark James, Sam Leach, Catherine Lewis-Morris, Catherine McBride, Rob McDonald, Benji McNair-Scott, Hayley Matthews, Alan Maxwell, Ian Pallent, Diana Rees-Jones, Lydia Richmond, Amy Robinson, Tiffer Robinson, Alistair Rycroft, Eddie Scrase-Field, Harry Steele, Brian Streeter, Hannah Sutcliffe, Julia Taylor, Mike Thompson, Andrew Vaughan, Robert Wynford-Harris, Tim Yau.

About Ridley Hall

Ridley Hall is an Anglican Theological College which in recent years has expanded its activities very considerably. The diagram below shows the range of these.

Working clockwise from the top:

Ordination training is the foundation task of the College. In the very recent past the College has joined with two major London parishes and their new Theological Centres to add a new form of mixed-mode training to the longer established two- and three-year residential training pattern. It is likely this method of training pioneer mission ministers will expand.

Lay training is delivered in two programmes other than the Faith in Business initiative dealt with separately below. Three courses a year are held for **Licensed Lay Ministers**. Delegates come from all over the country for the 3-day programmes in April and September which are called 'Resource & Refresh'. Details can be obtained from *The R&R Administrator, Ridley Hall, Cambridge, CB3 9HG.* **For people who want lay training that is more intensive and full time** it is possible to study alongside the ordinands to gain a Certificate in Mission and Evangelism Studies. The modules that make up the Certificate are taken from the first two levels of the BA Degree in Christian Theology and leave open the possibility of further study to diploma or degree level. If you are interested in this possibility, please write to *Dr Paul Weston, Tutor in Mission Studies, Ridley Hall, Cambridge, CB3 9HG.*

Theology Through the Arts is run by Revd Professor Jeremy Begbie. It is a project that engages with the world's growing artistic ferment. It aims to show how the arts of our time can help us discover and explore the riches of the Christian faith. More information can be found on the website (www.theolarts.org).

Sabbatical and Study Leave Programmes are available for those in full-time ministry – contact *Revd Prof Jeremy Begbie, Ridley Hall, Cambridge, CB3 9HG.*

Youth and Community Work training is provided by The Centre for Youth Ministry. It is possible to study for a BA honours degree in Youth and Community Work and Applied

Theology. The course is validated by Oxford Brookes University and the National Youth Agency (JNC). Plans are at an advanced stage for an MA course for youth work practitioners and to extend the current programme to incorporate children's work. More information from *CYM, Ridley Hall, Cambridge CB3 9HG* or visit the website (www.centreforyouthministry.ac.uk).

International links are varied, with students from all over the world training at the College. Recently (November 2006) a student exchange has been made with Al Azhar University in Cairo in an important Christian/Islamic programme in conjunction with the Divinity Faculty of Cambridge University.

Faith in Business: seminars are provided for business people who wish to explore the links between their faith and the way they conduct business. For up-to-date information go to the website (www.ridley.cam.ac.uk) and follow the drop-down menu or write to *Dr Richard Higginson, Ridley Hall, Cambridge, CB3 9HG.*

Further information on all these opportunities can be found at **www.ridley.cam.ac.uk**

If you would like to receive the College's latest **Annual Newsletter** please write to *The Development Office, Ridley Hall, Cambridge, CB3 9HG.*

The recent history of Ridley Hall has been one of constant development and the College is heavily dependent on voluntary gifts to maintain the necessary pace of change to train Christian leaders for the twenty-first century to the highest standard possible.

If you have found this book helpful and would like to contribute to the work of the College please send a gift to *The Development Office, Ridley Hall, Cambridge CB3 9HG*. It will be greatly appreciated. The Development Officer, Trevor Thorn, would also be very pleased to hear from anyone who might be minded to leave a legacy to the College. This can be discussed with Trevor in confidence on 01223 741069.

Ridley Hall is a registered charity – number 311456.

Ridley Hall is home to Grove Books, publishers of 28-page explorations of Christian life and ministry, covering a wide range of topics, from fair trade to forgiveness and from mission strategy to marriage. Booklets cost just £2.95 each, and are written by practitioners, not theorists, in eight series: Biblical, Ethics, Evangelism, Pastoral, Renewal, Spirituality, Worship and Youth.

Call 01223 464748 for a stocklist or visit the Grove website (www.grovebooks.co.uk).